P9-DMU-312

Fairy Tale Science

Growing a Beanstalk for Jack

by Joanne Mattern

Whiting Public Library
Whiting, Indiana

FOCUS
READERS.

BEACON

www.focusreaders.com

Copyright © 2020 by Focus Readers®, Lake Elmo, MN 55042. All rights reserved. No part of this book may be reproduced or utilized in any form or by any means without written permission from the publisher.

Focus Readers is distributed by North Star Editions:
sales@northstareditions.com | 888-417-0195

Produced for Focus Readers by Red Line Editorial.

Photographs ©: ClassicStock/Alamy, cover (left), 1 (left); Red Line Editorial, cover (right), 1 (right), 11, 13, 15, 16–17, 27; Elena Sherengovskaya/Shutterstock Images, 4, 29; sarahlouisephotography/ iStockphoto, 7; Mathia Coco/Shutterstock Images, 8; Yala/Shutterstock Images, 18; BogWan/ iStockphoto, 21; iShootPhotosLLC/iStockphoto, 22; Bess Hamitii/Shutterstock Images, 25

Library of Congress Cataloging-in-Publication Data
Names: Mattern, Joanne, 1963- author.
Title: Growing a beanstalk for Jack / by Joanne Mattern.
Description: Lake Elmo, MN : Focus Readers, [2020] | Series: Fairy tale
  science | Includes index. | Audience: Grades 4–6.
Identifiers: LCCN 2019034735 (print) | LCCN 2019034736 (ebook) | ISBN
  9781644930274 (hardcover) | ISBN 9781644931066 (paperback) | ISBN
  9781644932643 (ebook pdf) | ISBN 9781644931851 (hosted ebook)
Subjects: LCSH: Beans--Juvenile literature. | Beans--Life cycles--Juvenile
  literature.
Classification: LCC SB327 .M38 2020 (print) | LCC SB327 (ebook) | DDC
  635/.65--dc23
LC record available at https://lccn.loc.gov/2019034735
LC ebook record available at https://lccn.loc.gov/2019034736

Printed in the United States of America
Mankato, MN
012020

About the Author

Joanne Mattern is the author of more than 200 books for children. Her favorite topics include science, history, biography, and sports. She also loves fairy tales and spooky stories. Mattern lives in New York State with her husband, children, and several pets.

Table of Contents

Chapter 1

Jack and the Beanstalk

Jack and his mother were very poor. Jack's mother told him to sell their cow. Instead, he traded the cow for five magic beans. Jack's mother was angry. She threw the beans outside.

 Jack was supposed to get money for the cow at the market.

The next morning, Jack looked outside. A huge beanstalk had grown. Jack climbed the beanstalk. At the top, he found the home of a giant. The home was filled with treasure. Jack took a bag of gold. He carried it home.

Jack climbed the beanstalk again. This time, he stole a magic goose. It laid golden eggs. Another time, Jack grabbed a harp. But the harp could talk. It called for help. The giant chased Jack down the beanstalk.

 Jack sold the golden eggs at the market.

Jack grabbed an axe. He chopped down the huge beanstalk. The giant fell down with a crash. Jack and his mother were safe.

7

Chapter 2

Growing a Bean Plant

Huge beanstalks only appear in fairy tales. But you can grow your own bean plants at home. Different plants grow best under different **conditions**. These conditions include water, sunlight, and soil.

 People can grow green beans to eat.

For example, some plants need lots of water. Other plants need only a little. Similarly, some plants thrive in direct sunlight. Other plants grow well in indirect sunlight.

You will grow bean plants in different levels of sunlight. You will see which plant grows best over time.

Fun Fact

People have been growing beans for more than 6,000 years.

Materials

- Three 10-ounce (300-mL) cups

- Soil

- Bean seeds

- Water

Instructions

1. Fill a cup with soil. Make sure the soil is not packed too tightly.

2. Use your finger to make a 1-inch (2.5-cm) hole in the soil. Drop a seed into the hole.

3. Lightly brush soil over the seed to cover it.

Fun Fact

Beans are one of the fastest-growing plants in the world.

4. Repeat steps 1–3 with the other
two cups.

5. Add water to each cup until the soil is **moist** but not too wet.

6. Place one cup in a sunny window. Place the second cup farther inside the room. Place the third cup in a dark room or closet.

7. Check the plants daily. Add water when the soil feels dry.

8. Watch and wait for your plants to grow. Record the results. Which plant grows the fastest? Which plant grows the biggest?

Greenhouses

Many people grow plants outside in the sun. They grow plants in the spring and summer. But some people live in cold **climates**. And other people may want to grow plants during the winter. In the winter, it is too cold to grow plants outside. The plants would freeze. Instead, people grow plants inside a greenhouse.

A greenhouse is made of glass. The glass lets in lots of sunlight. The sunlight warms the inside of the greenhouse. The building traps the heat inside. The greenhouse stays warm and wet. It is a great place for plants to grow.

Heat from the sun enters the greenhouse.

The walls and roof trap some of the heat inside.

People can add plastic sheeting to trap even more heat inside.

Chapter 3

Results

The plant in direct sunlight grew very well. It grew full leaves. The plant in indirect sunlight grew, too. Its stem was long. The stem bent toward the nearest window. The plant in the dark also grew.

 Plants grow toward light.

Bean plants do not need sunlight to **germinate**. But this plant did not grow leaves. Its stem was long and white.

Try growing new bean plants while changing other conditions:

- Water one plant every day. Water another plant only when the soil is dry. Do not water the

Fun Fact

The color of the light can also affect how plants grow.

 Changes happen underground before a plant breaks through to the surface.

third plant at all. Which plant grows best?

- Place one seed in sand. Place another seed in soil. Place the third seed in clay. Which plant grows best?

Chapter 4

The Science Behind Plants

Most plants have the same parts. Those parts are seeds, roots, stems, leaves, and flowers. When a seed germinates, roots grow down into the soil. They soak up **nutrients** and water in the soil.

 Even though they look very different, most plants have the same parts.

Soon a stem grows out of the seed. The stem pushes up through the soil. It holds up the plant.

In time, the stem grows leaves. Leaves help make food for the plant. Later, the plant grows flowers. Flowers hold new seeds. These seeds fall to the ground. They get buried in the soil. The cycle of life starts all over again.

Plants get nutrients from the soil. But plants also make their own food. This process is called

 The wind blows dandelion seeds to new areas. Soon new dandelions will grow.

photosynthesis. The process starts with water, air, and sunlight.

Plants absorb water from the soil. They also take in a gas called carbon dioxide from the air. **Chlorophyll** in leaves absorbs sunlight. That light has **energy**.

Plants use that energy. They change the carbon dioxide and water into **oxygen** and glucose. Glucose is food for the plant. Plants release the oxygen into the air.

People and animals breathe in the oxygen. We need oxygen to live. Without plants, there would be no oxygen for people to breathe. Plants

Fun Fact

Chlorophyll is what gives leaves their green color.

PHOTOSYNTHESIS

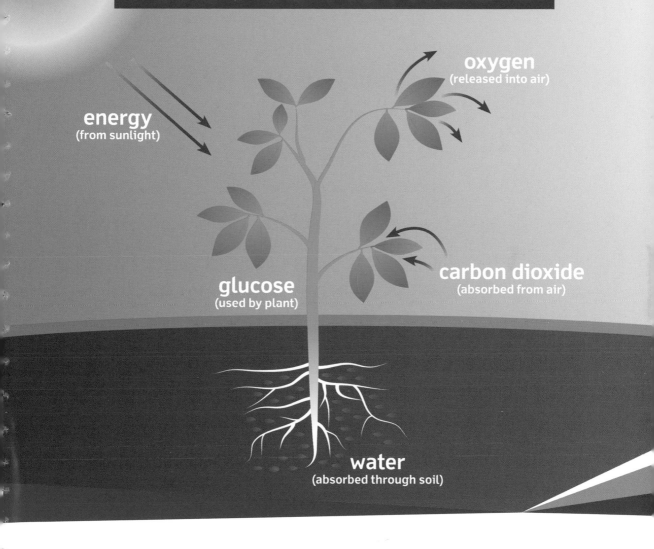

energy
(from sunlight)

oxygen
(released into air)

carbon dioxide
(absorbed from air)

glucose
(used by plant)

water
(absorbed through soil)

might not take us up to a giant's castle. But without them, there would be no life on Earth.

FOCUS ON
Growing a Beanstalk

Write your answers on a separate piece of paper.

1. Write a paragraph that summarizes the main idea of Chapter 3.

2. Do you think it is easy to grow healthy plants? Why or why not?

3. Why did the plant in the window grow the best?
   - **A.** It received the most sunlight.
   - **B.** It received the most water.
   - **C.** It received the most fresh air.

4. What might happen to a plant if the soil is packed very tightly?
   - **A.** The plant will grow faster and better.
   - **B.** The plant's roots will not be able to grow as well.
   - **C.** The plant's leaves will not be able to take in sunlight.

5. What does **thrive** mean in this book?

*Similarly, some plants **thrive** in direct sunlight. Other plants grow well in indirect sunlight.*

    A. turn white

    B. die or become ill

    C. develop quickly

6. What does **absorb** mean in this book?

*Plants **absorb** water from the soil. They also take in a gas called carbon dioxide from the air.*

    A. give off

    B. soak up

    C. get rid of

Answer key on page 32.

Whiting Public Library
Whiting, Indiana

Glossary

chlorophyll
A green chemical that allows plants to absorb sunlight.

climates
The average weather conditions of particular places or regions.

conditions
Parts of an environment that affect how things live.

energy
The ability to do work.

germinate
To begin to grow.

moist
A little wet or damp.

nutrients
Substances that humans, animals, and plants need to stay strong and healthy.

oxygen
A gas in the air that humans and animals need to breathe to survive.

photosynthesis
The process in which plants turn sunlight, carbon dioxide, and water into glucose and oxygen.

To Learn More

BOOKS

Amstutz, Lisa J. *Investigating Plant Life Cycles.* Minneapolis: Lerner Publications, 2016.

Ringstad, Arnold. *The Plant Life Cycle.* Mankato, MN: The Child's World, 2019.

Royston, Angela. *What Do You Know About Plants?* New York: PowerKids Press, 2018.

NOTE TO EDUCATORS

Visit **www.focusreaders.com** to find lesson plans, activities, links, and other resources related to this title.

Index

B

beans, 5, 10, 12

C

carbon dioxide, 25–27
chlorophyll, 25–26
climates, 16

F

flowers, 23–24

G

glucose, 26–27
greenhouse, 16–17

J

Jack, 5–7

L

leaves, 19–20, 23–26

N

nutrients, 23–24

O

oxygen, 26–27

P

photosynthesis, 25, 27

R

roots, 23

S

seeds, 11–12, 21, 23–24
soil, 9, 11–12, 14, 20–21,
    23–25, 27
stems, 19–20, 23–24
sunlight, 9–10, 16, 19–20,
    25, 27

W

water, 9–11, 14, 20, 23,
    25–27

Answer Key: 1. Answers will vary; **2.** Answers will vary; **3.** A; **4.** B; **5.** C; **6.** B